Barb And Her Camera

Birds and Blooms

Barbara Hamp-Weicksel

ISBN:1494285088
ISBN-13:9781494285081

For those who see the world through the eye of their camera.
And to those who patiently wait for us to catch up –

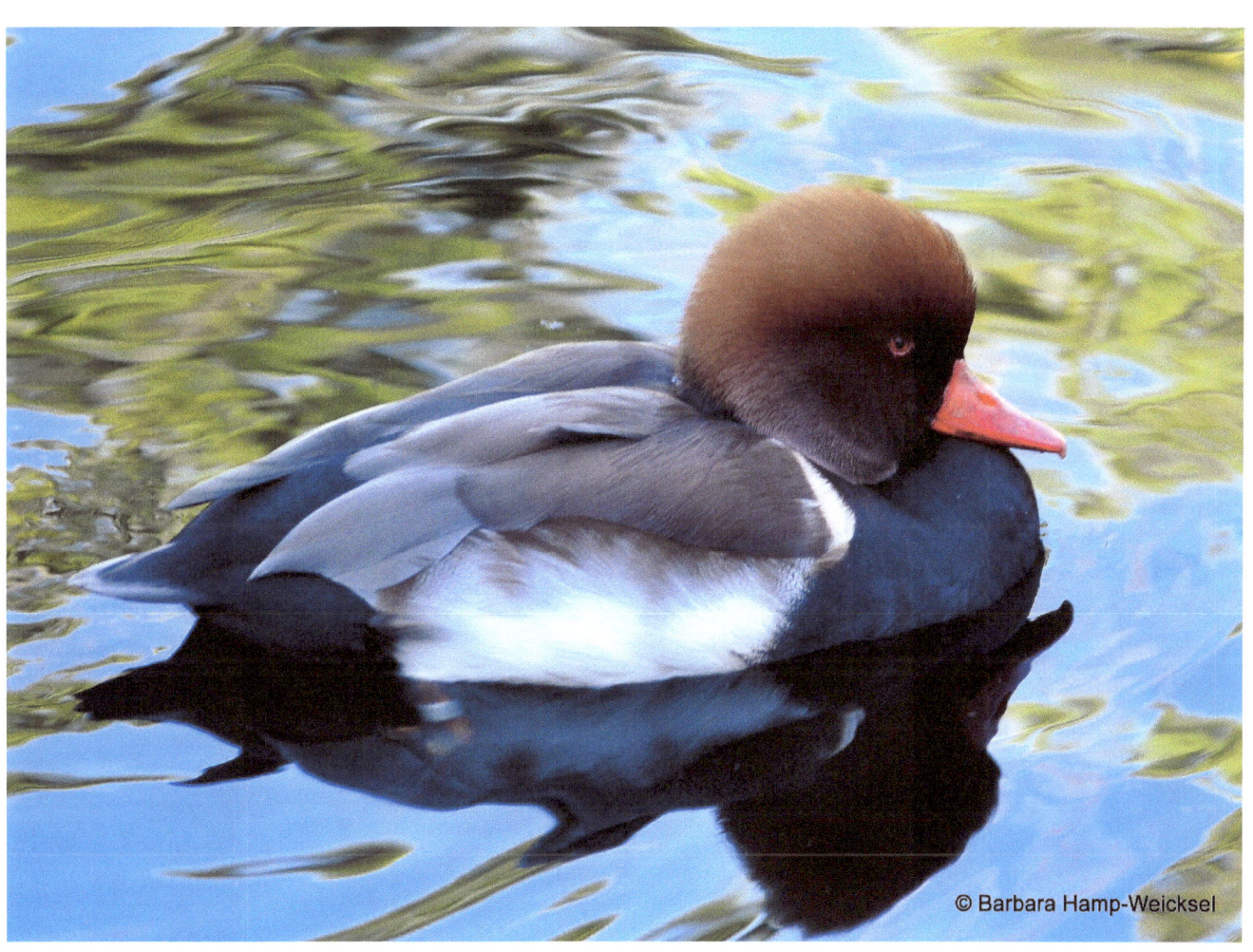

© Barbara Hamp-Weicksel

ACKNOWLEDGMENTS

My thanks to my neighbors who understand when they see me in their flower beds or sitting in their front yards watching and photographing the birds.

Barb And Her Camera

Birds and Blooms

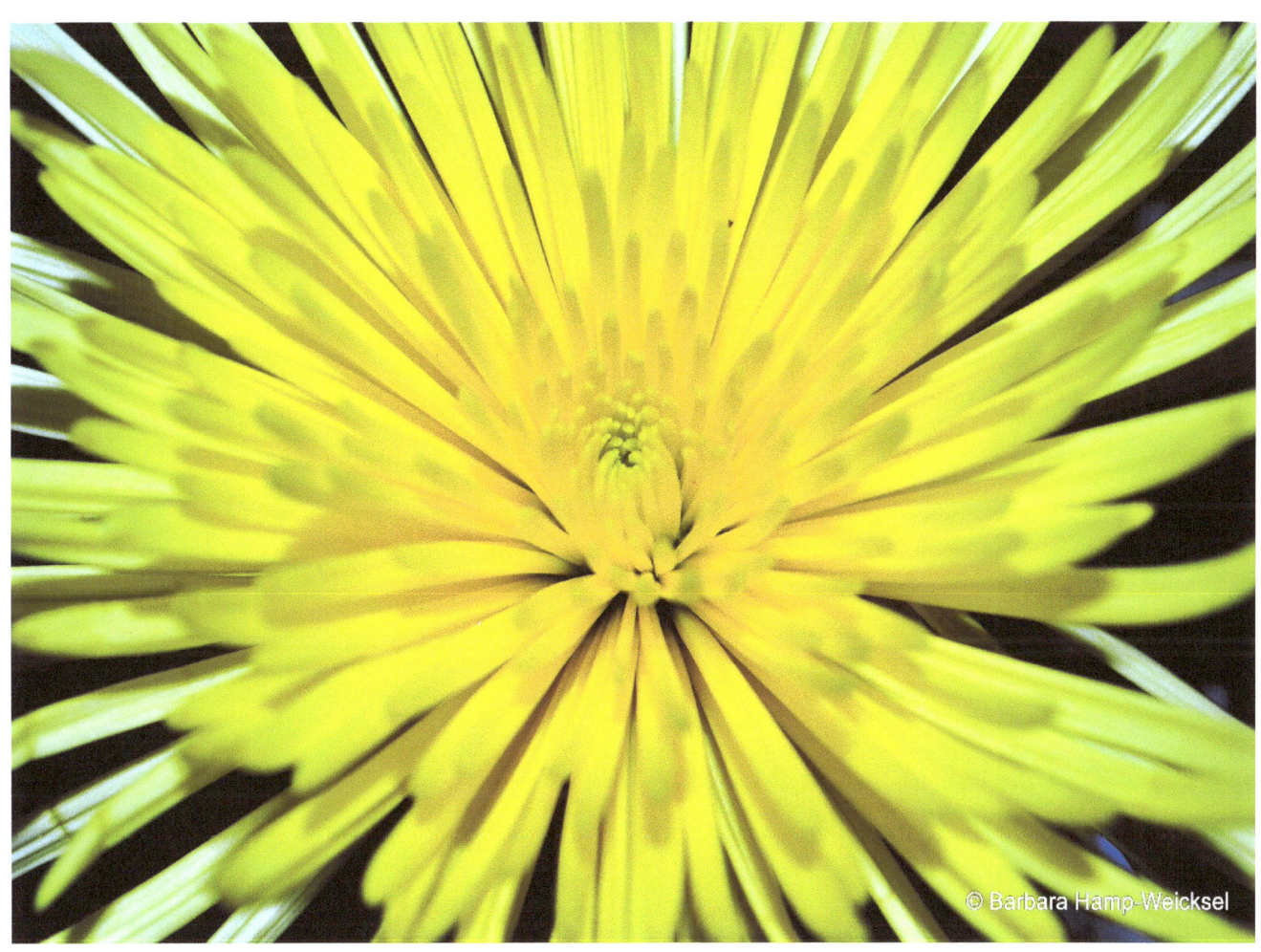

© Barbara Hamp-Weicksel

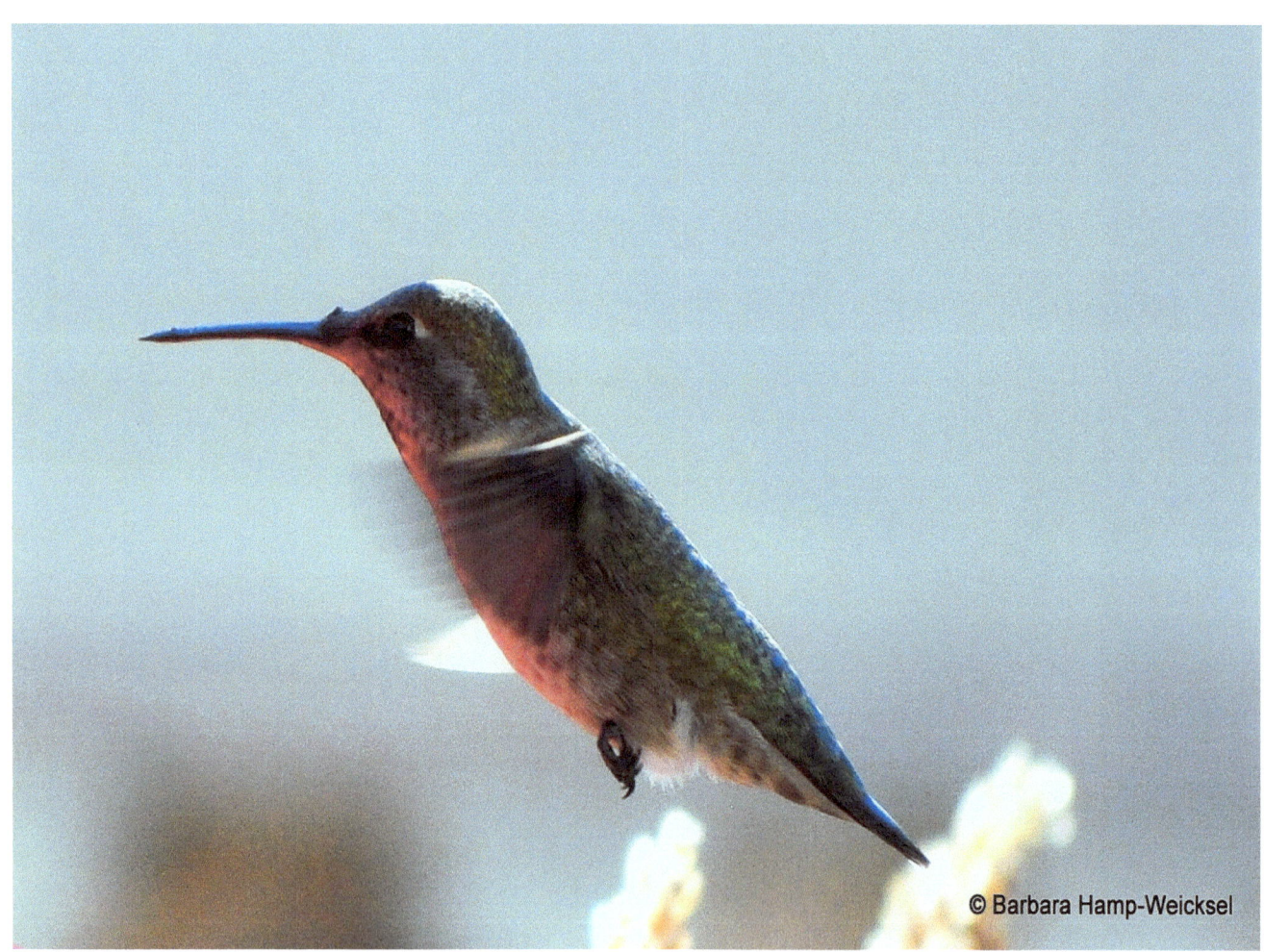

© Barbara Hamp-Weicksel

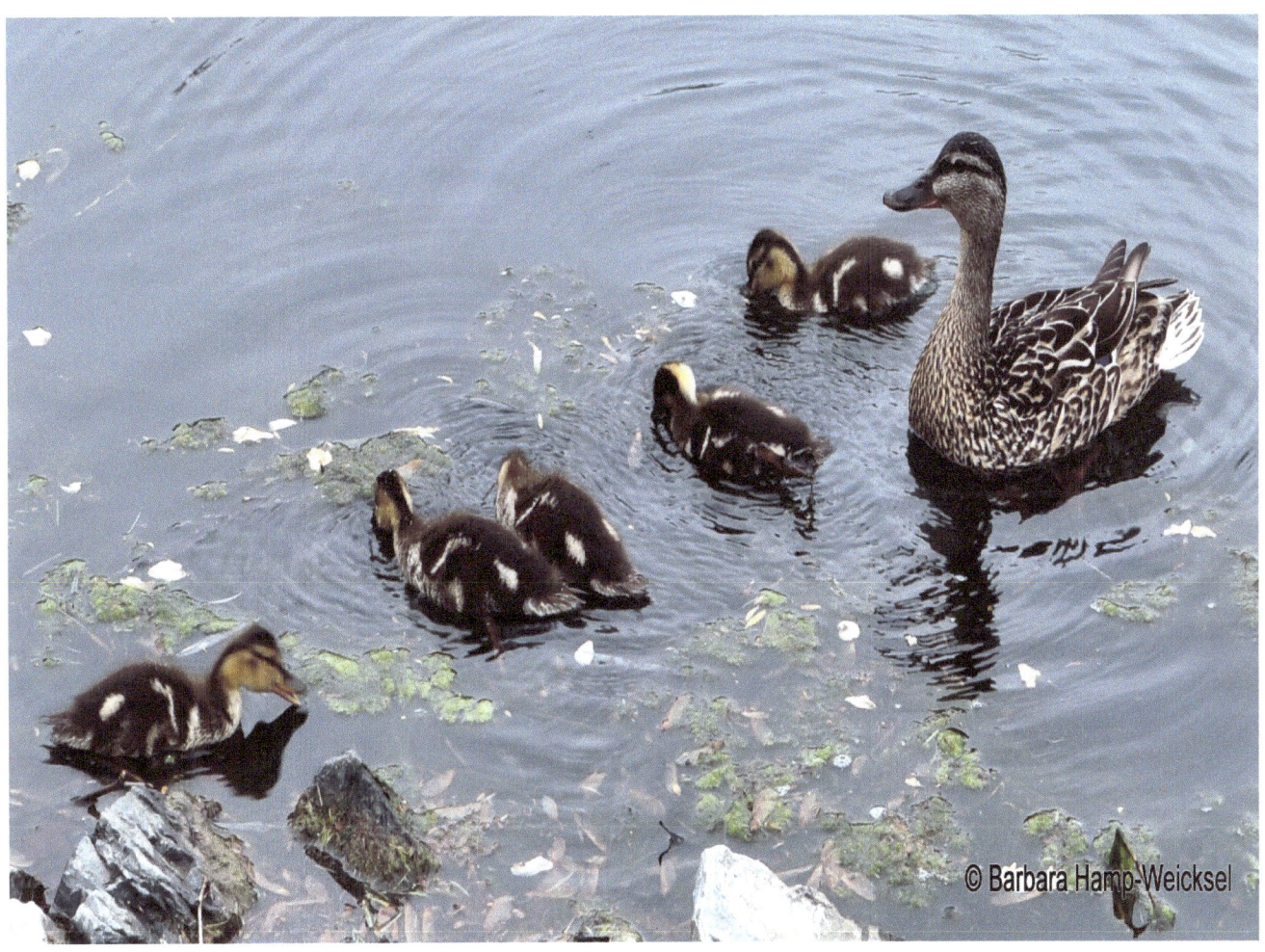

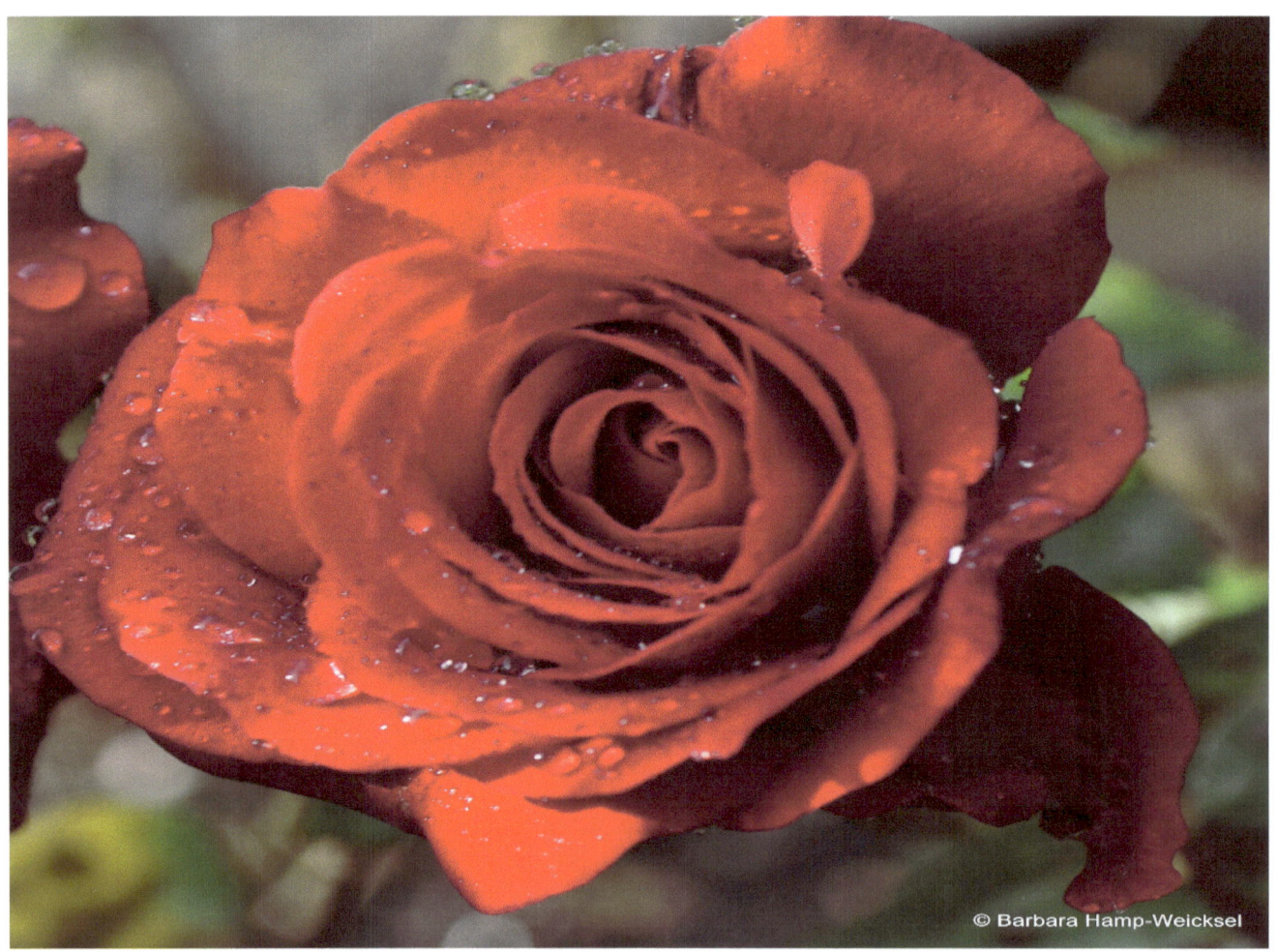

© Barbara Hamp-Weicksel

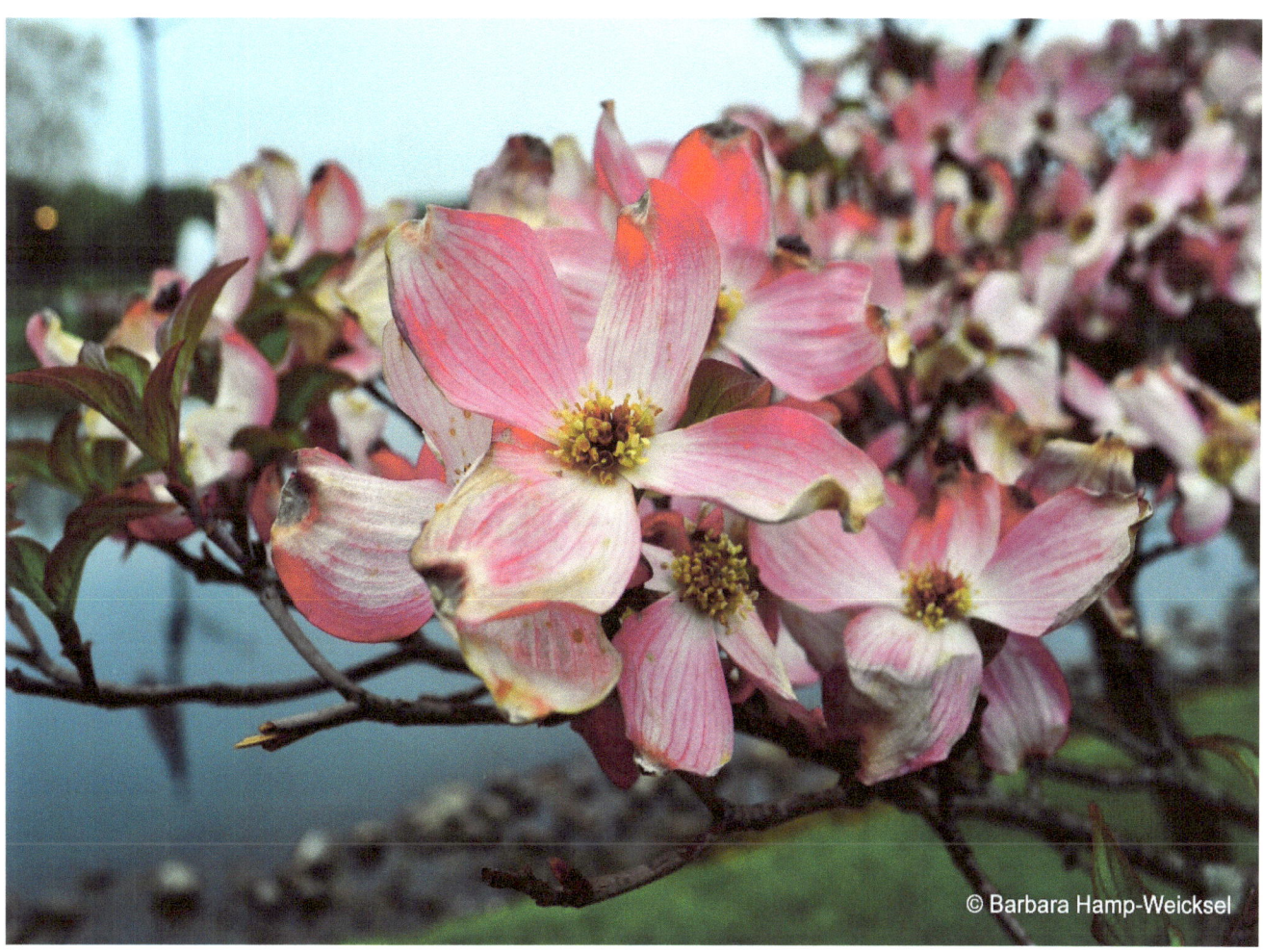

© Barbara Hamp-Weicksel

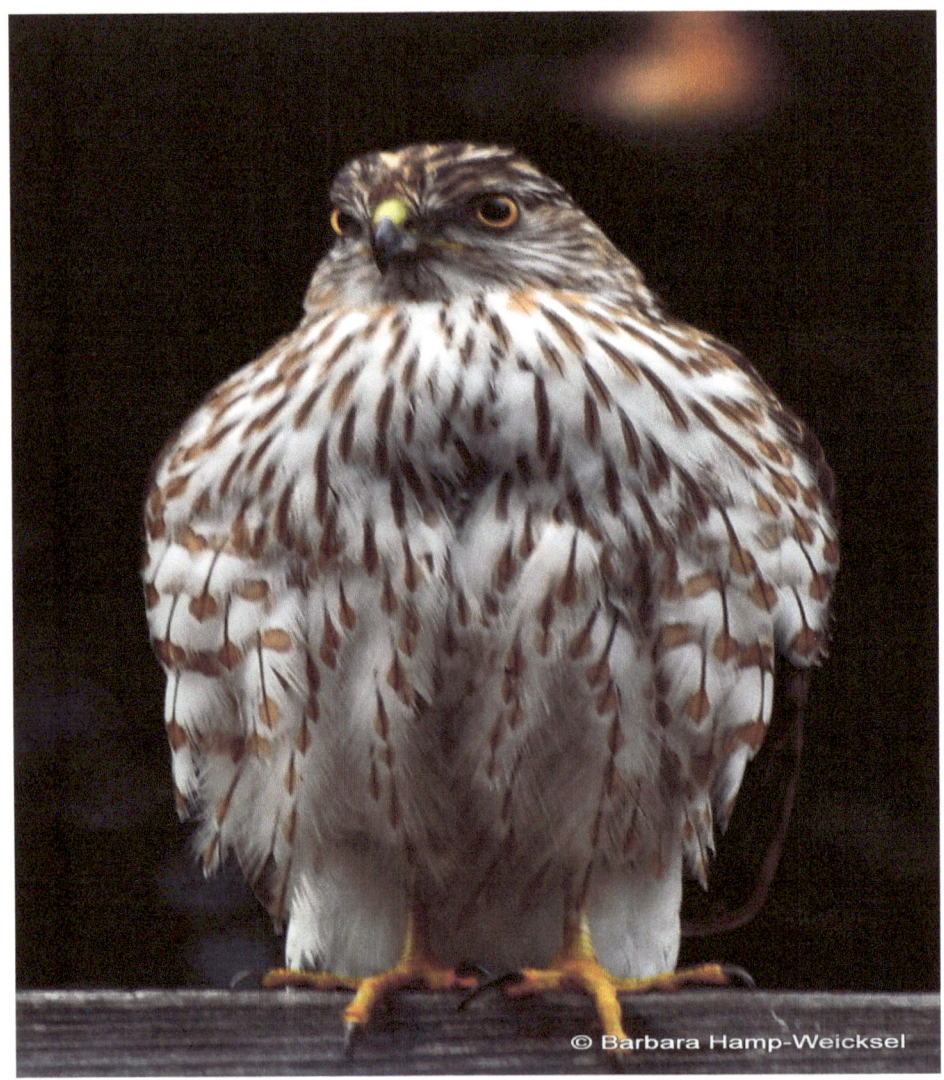

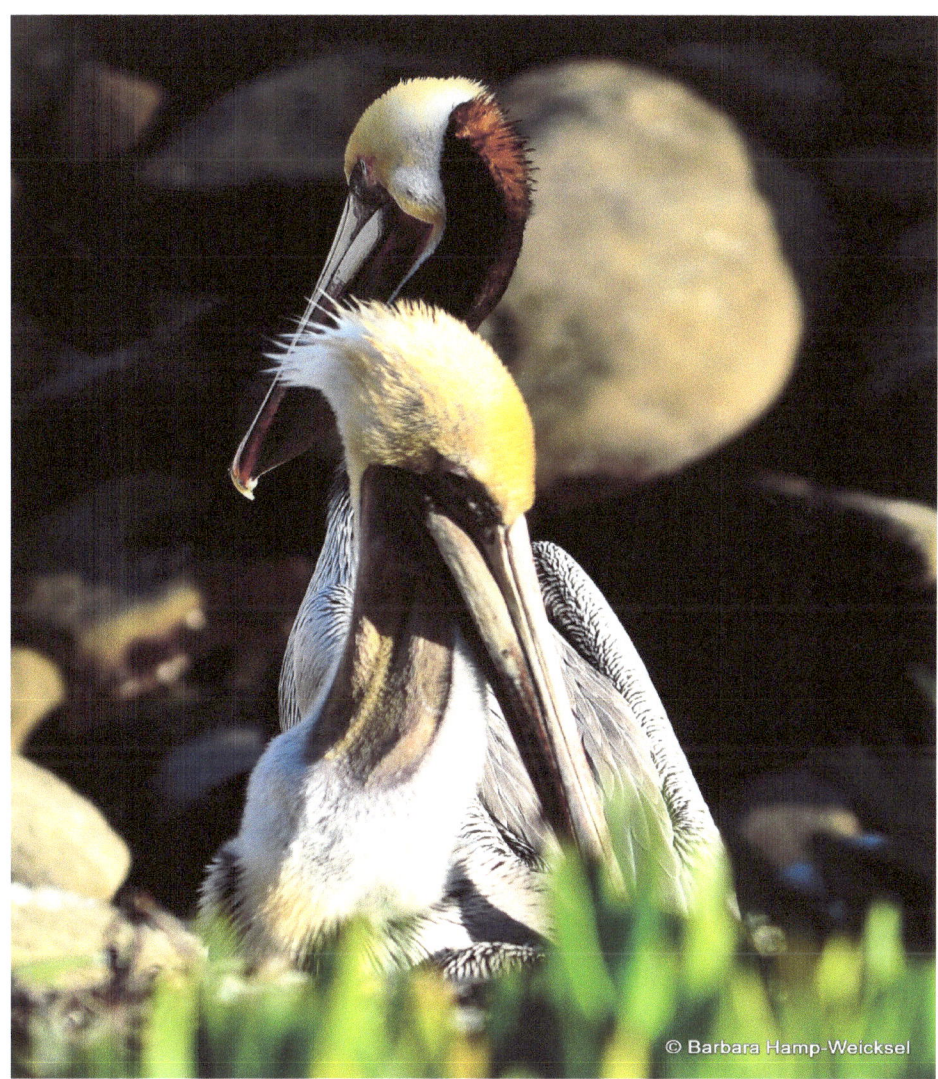

© Barbara Hamp-Weicksel

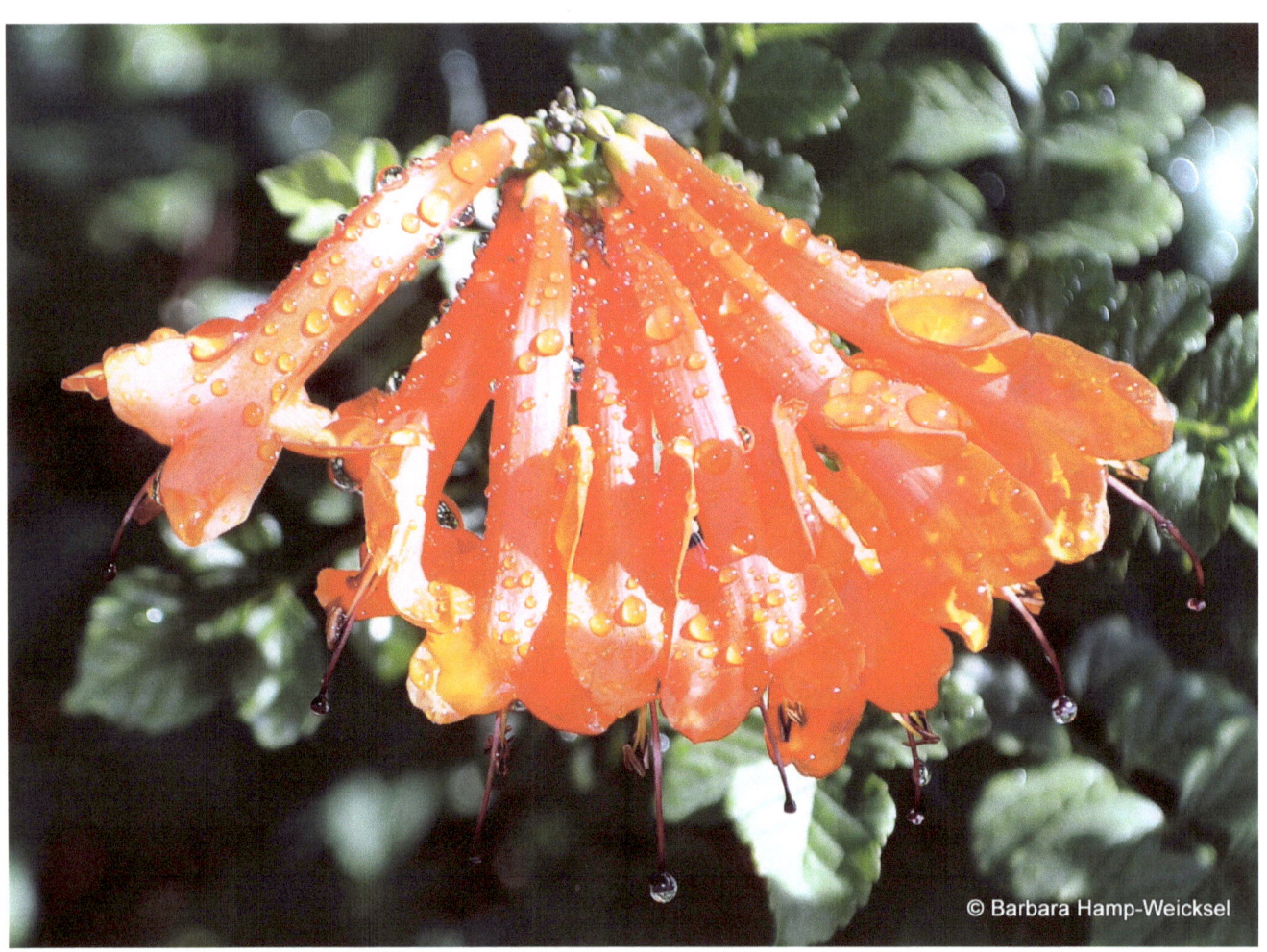

© Barbara Hamp-Weicksel

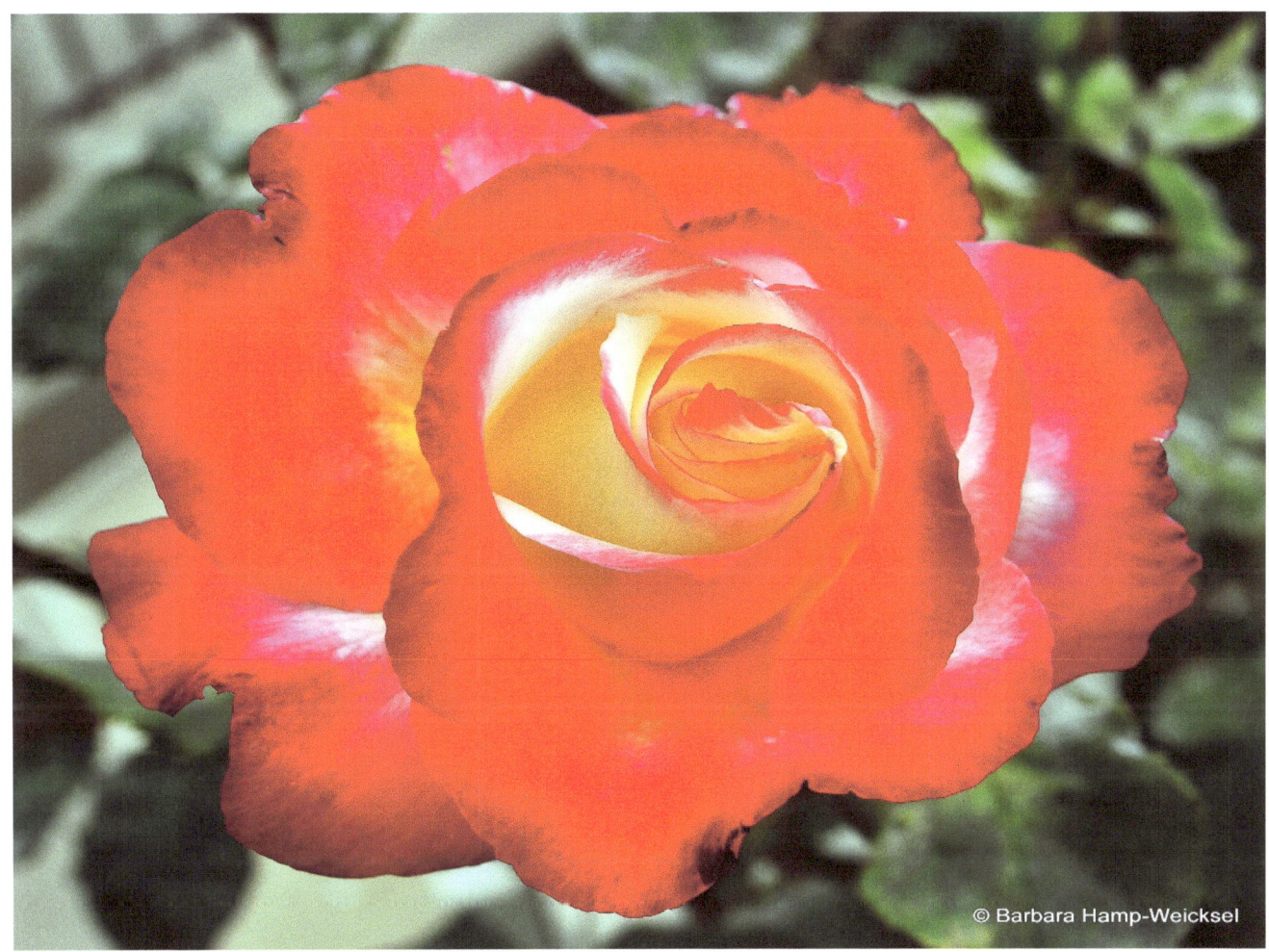

© Barbara Hamp-Weicksel

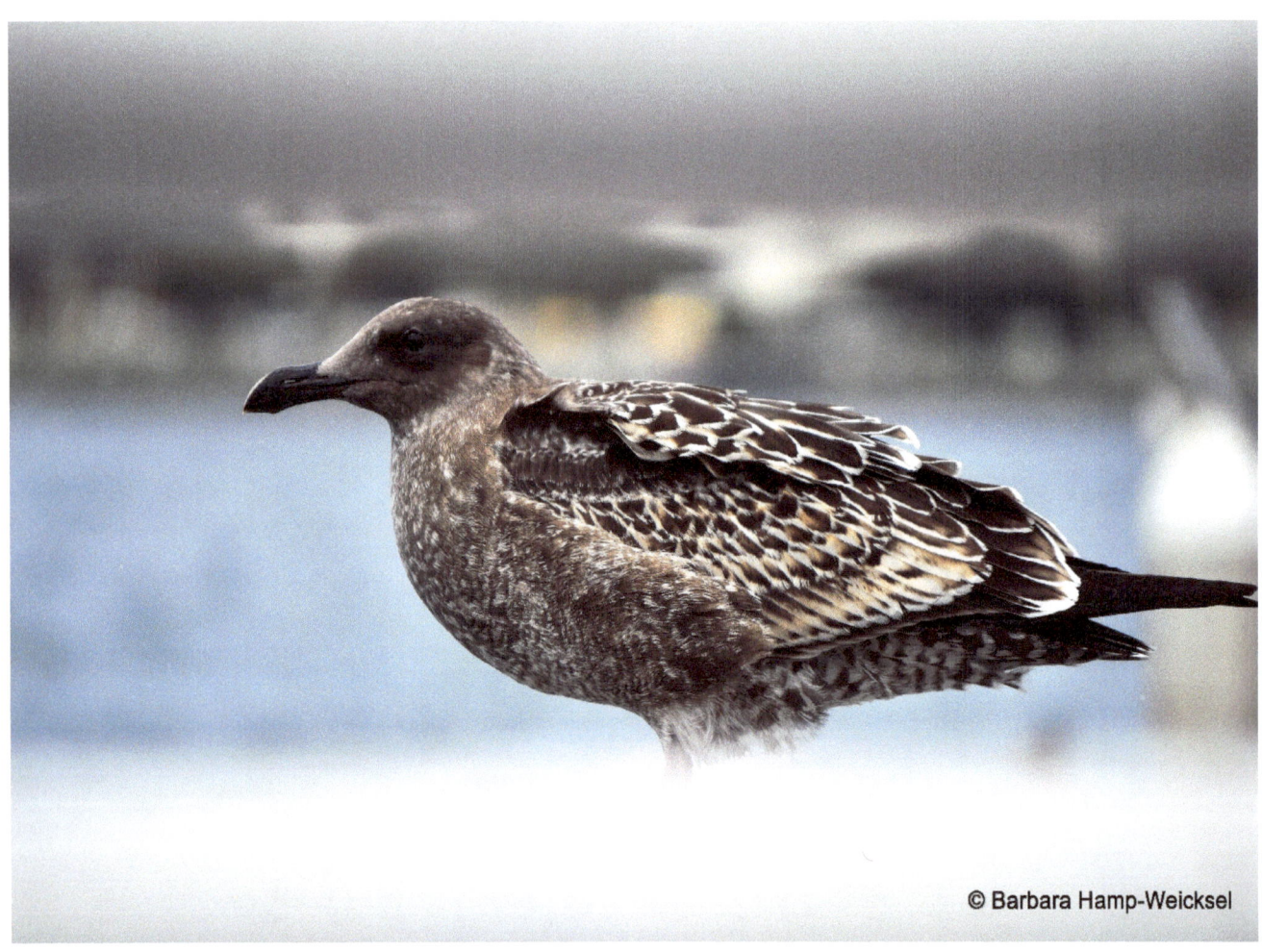

© Barbara Hamp-Weicksel

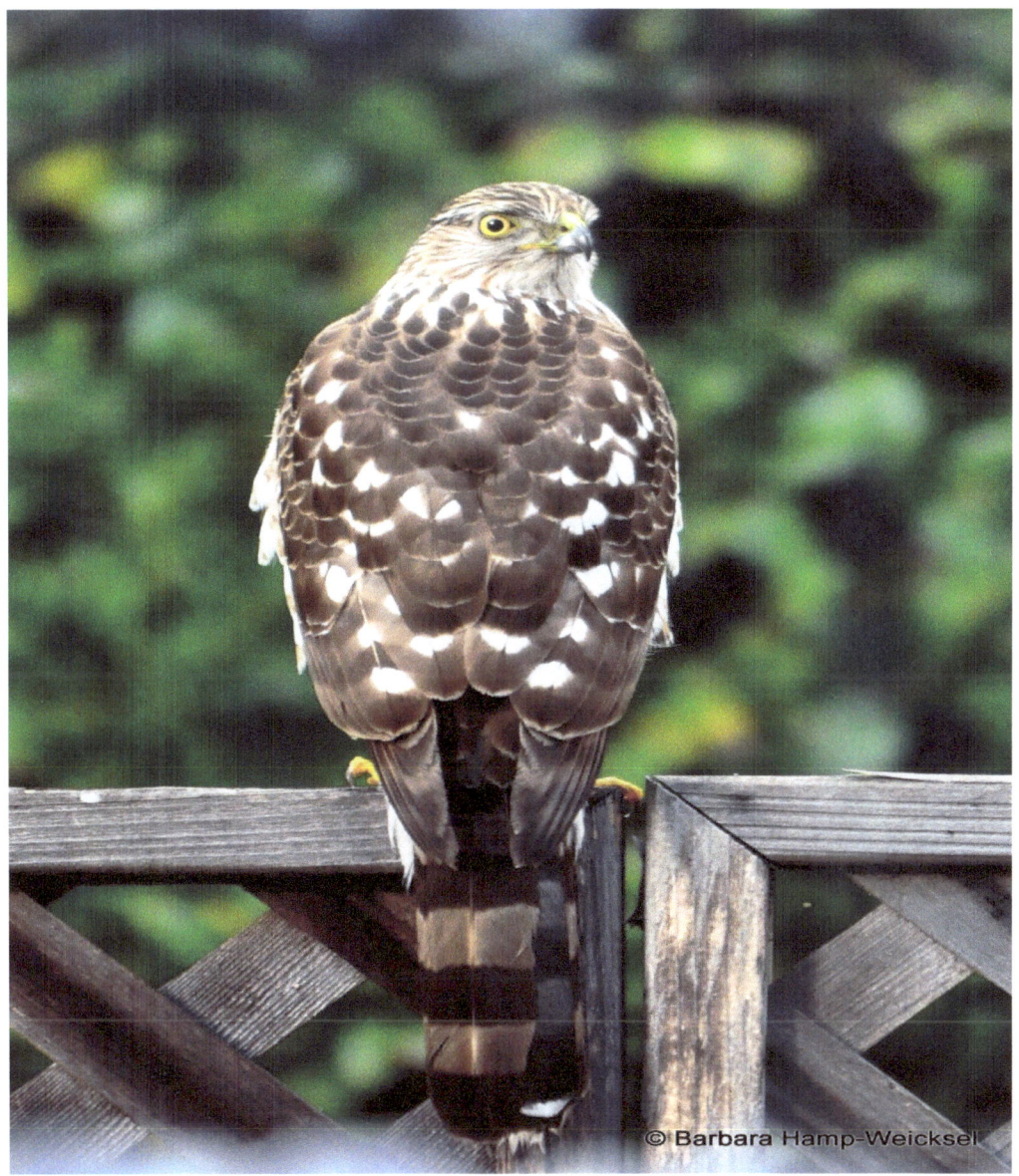

Barbara Hamp-Weicksel

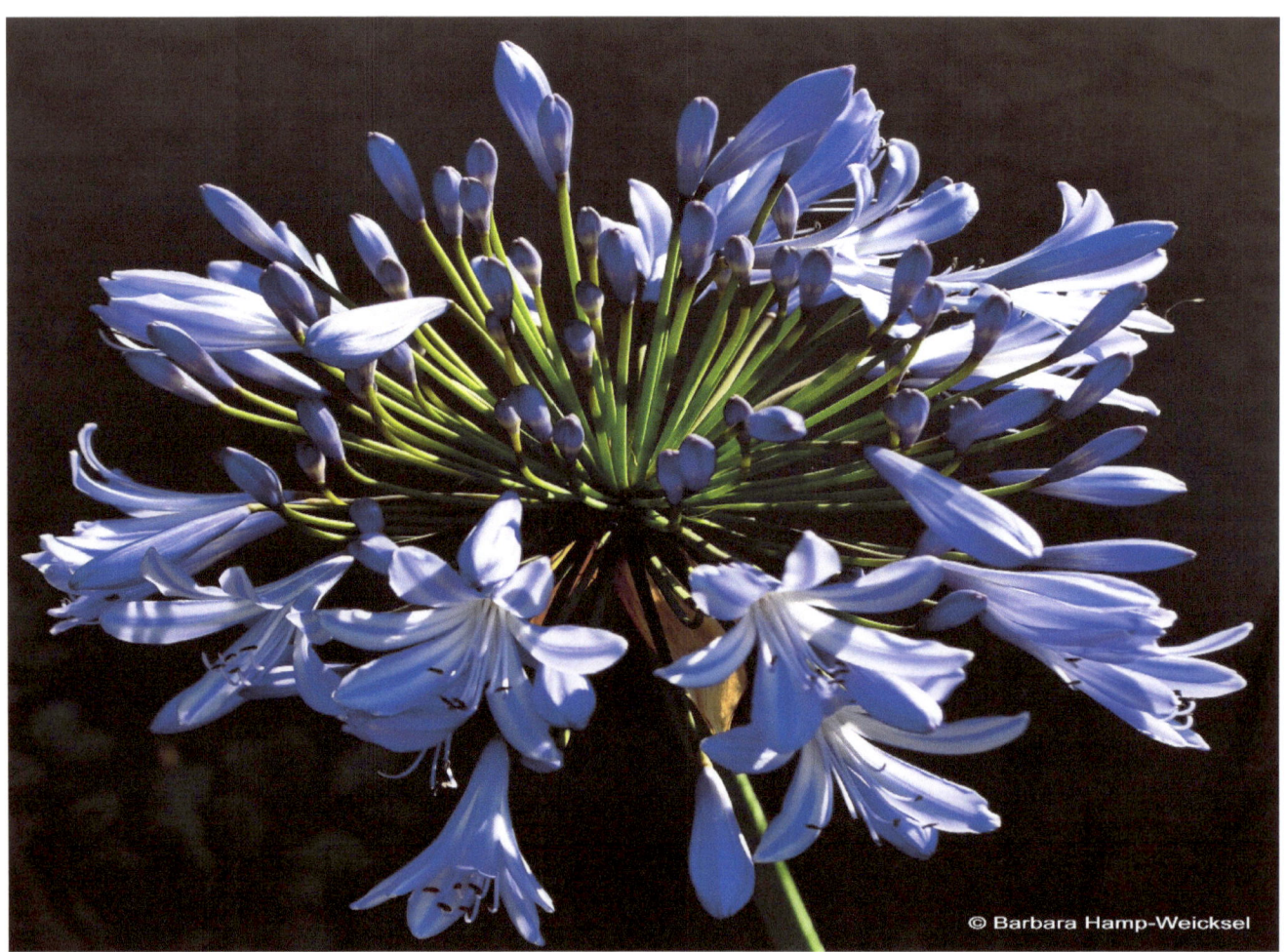

© Barbara Hamp-Weicksel

14

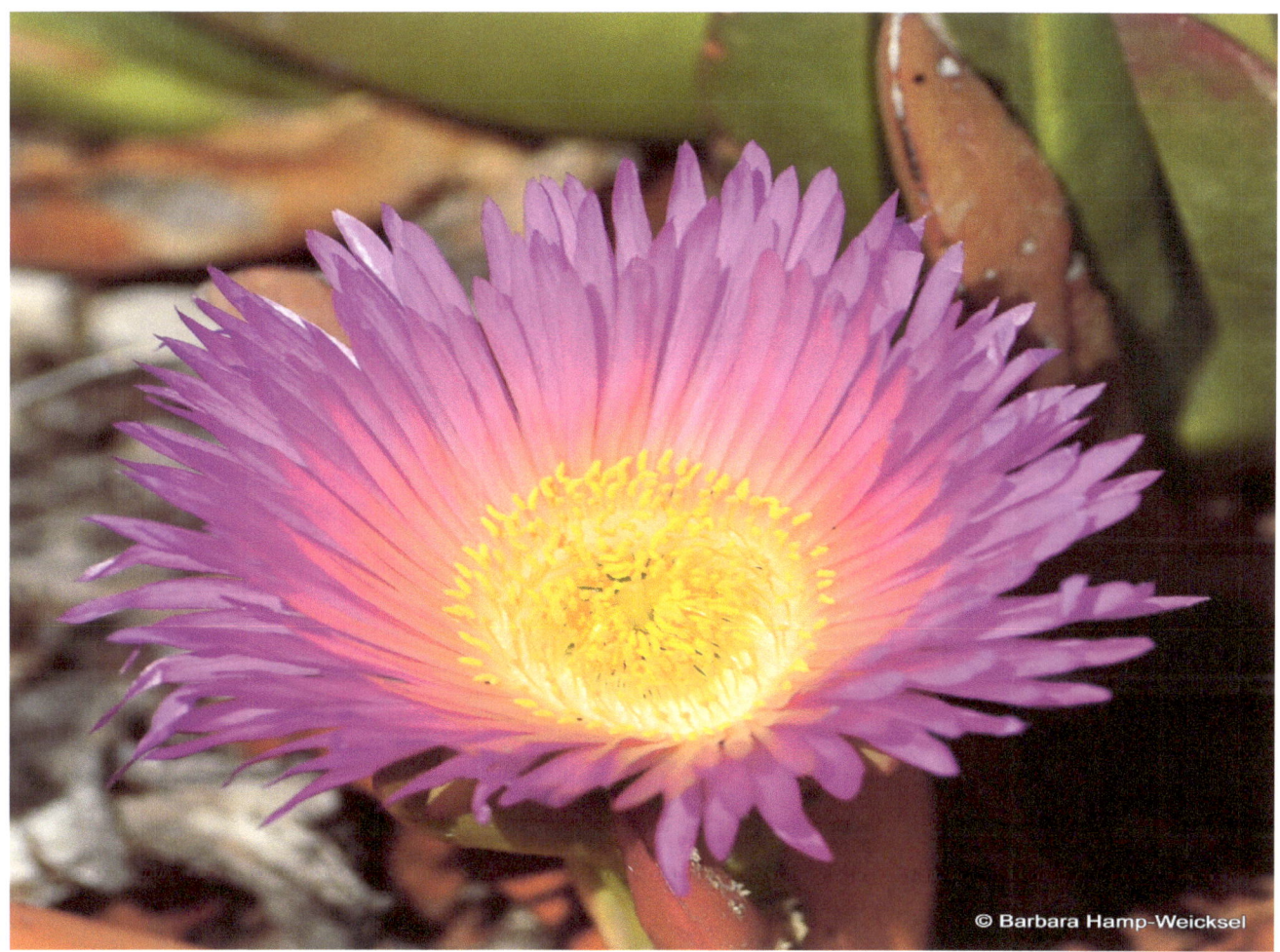

© Barbara Hamp-Weicksel

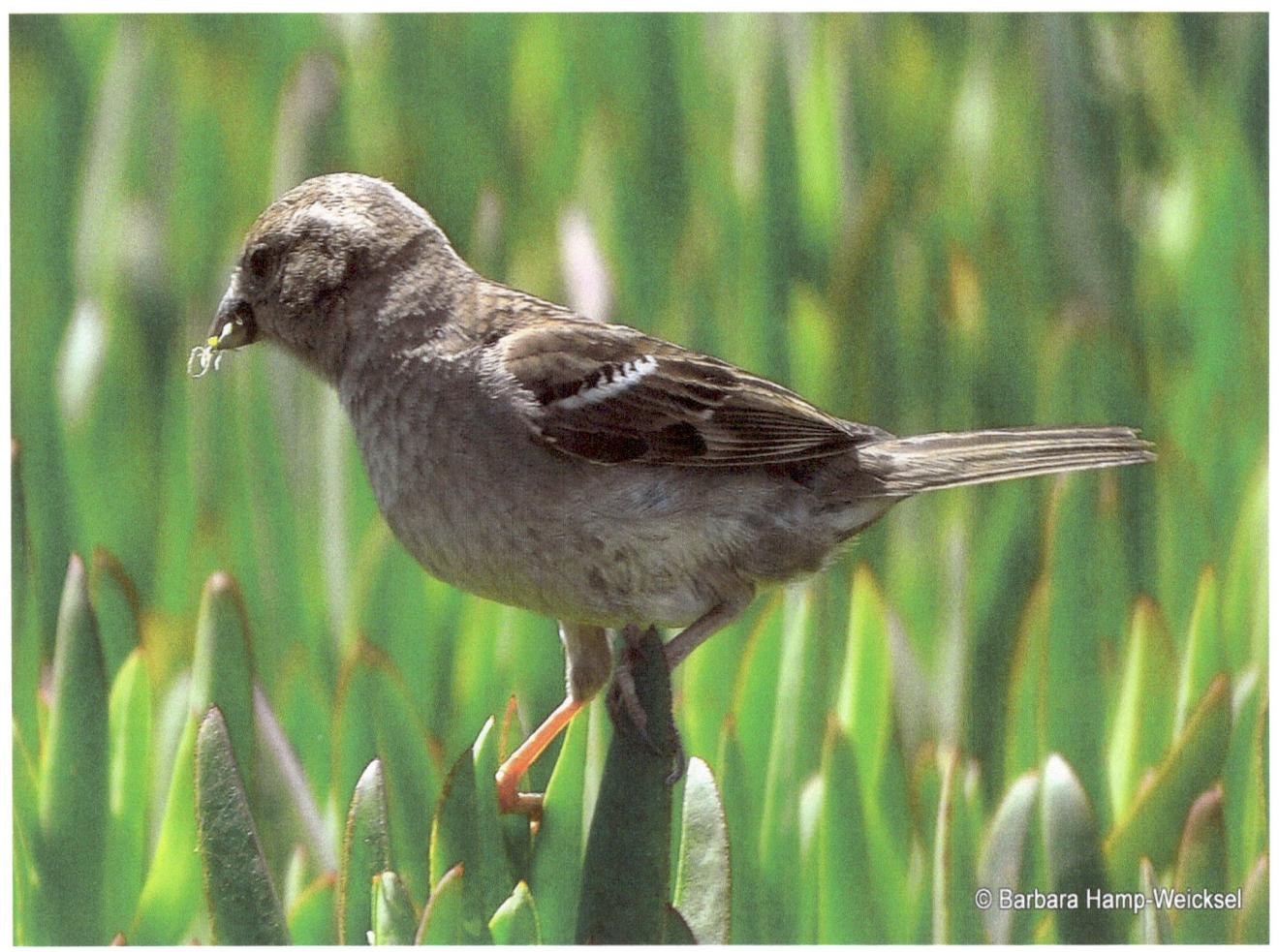

© Barbara Hamp-Weicksel

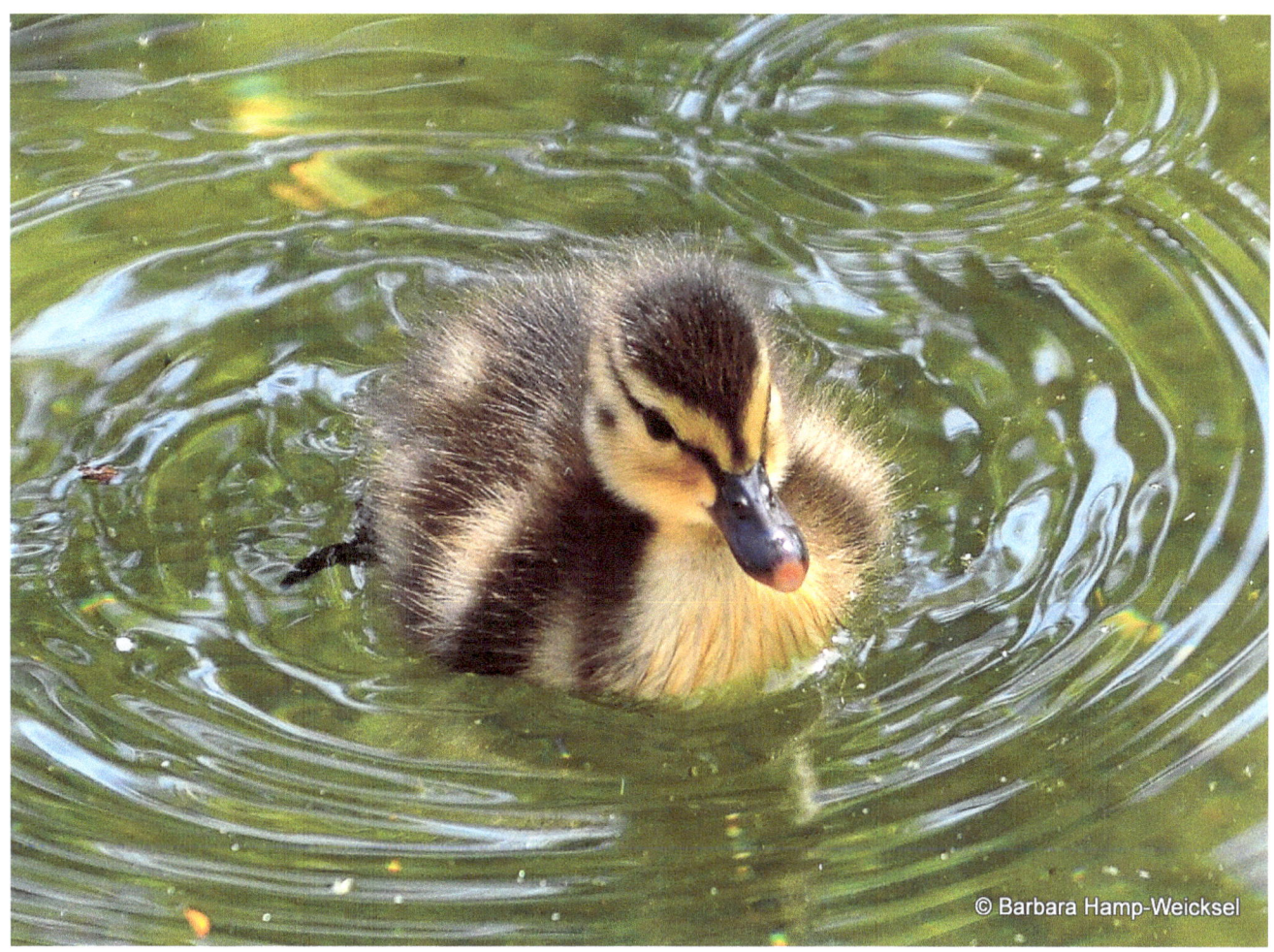

© Barbara Hamp-Weicksel

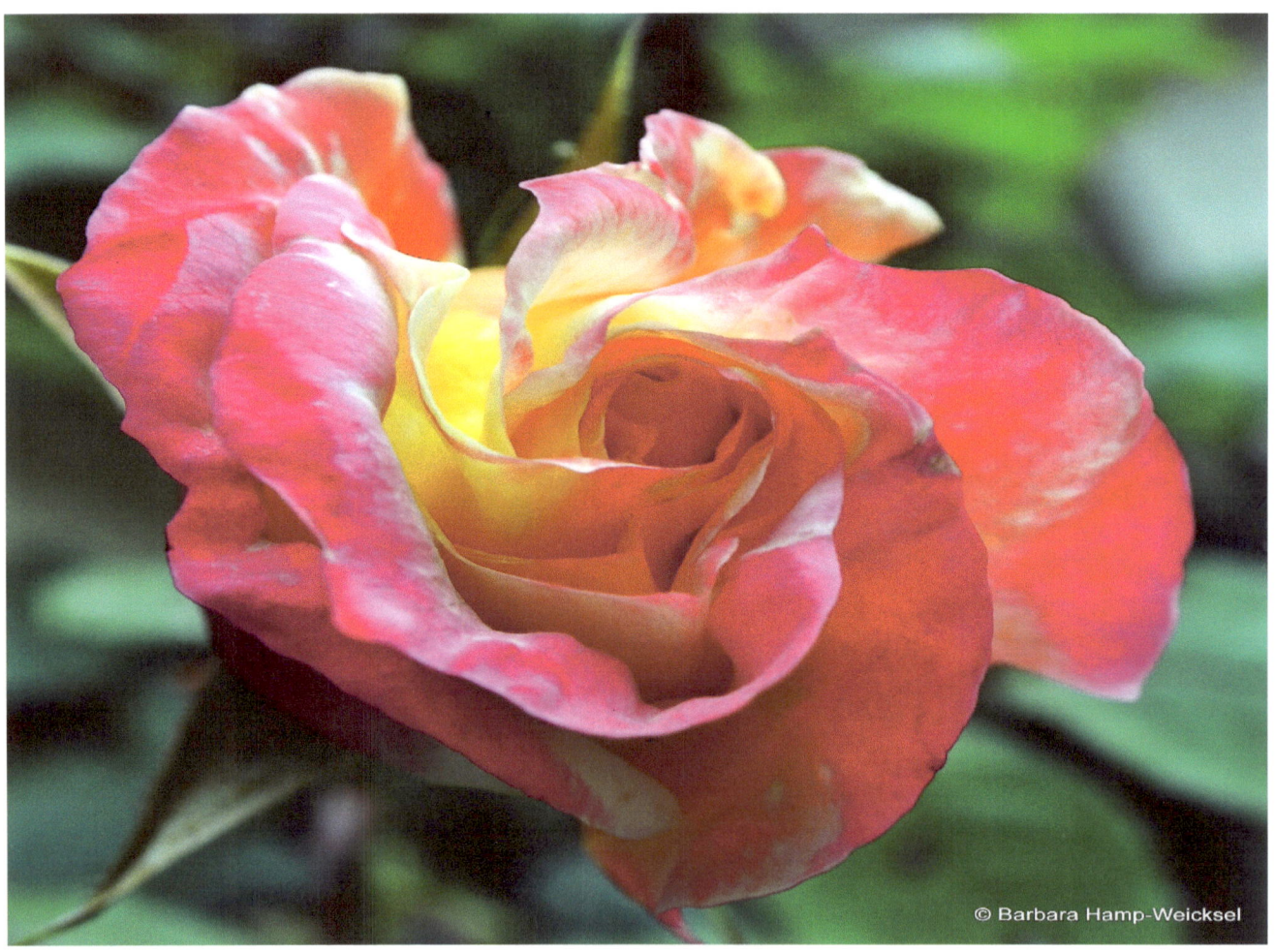

© Barbara Hamp-Weicksel

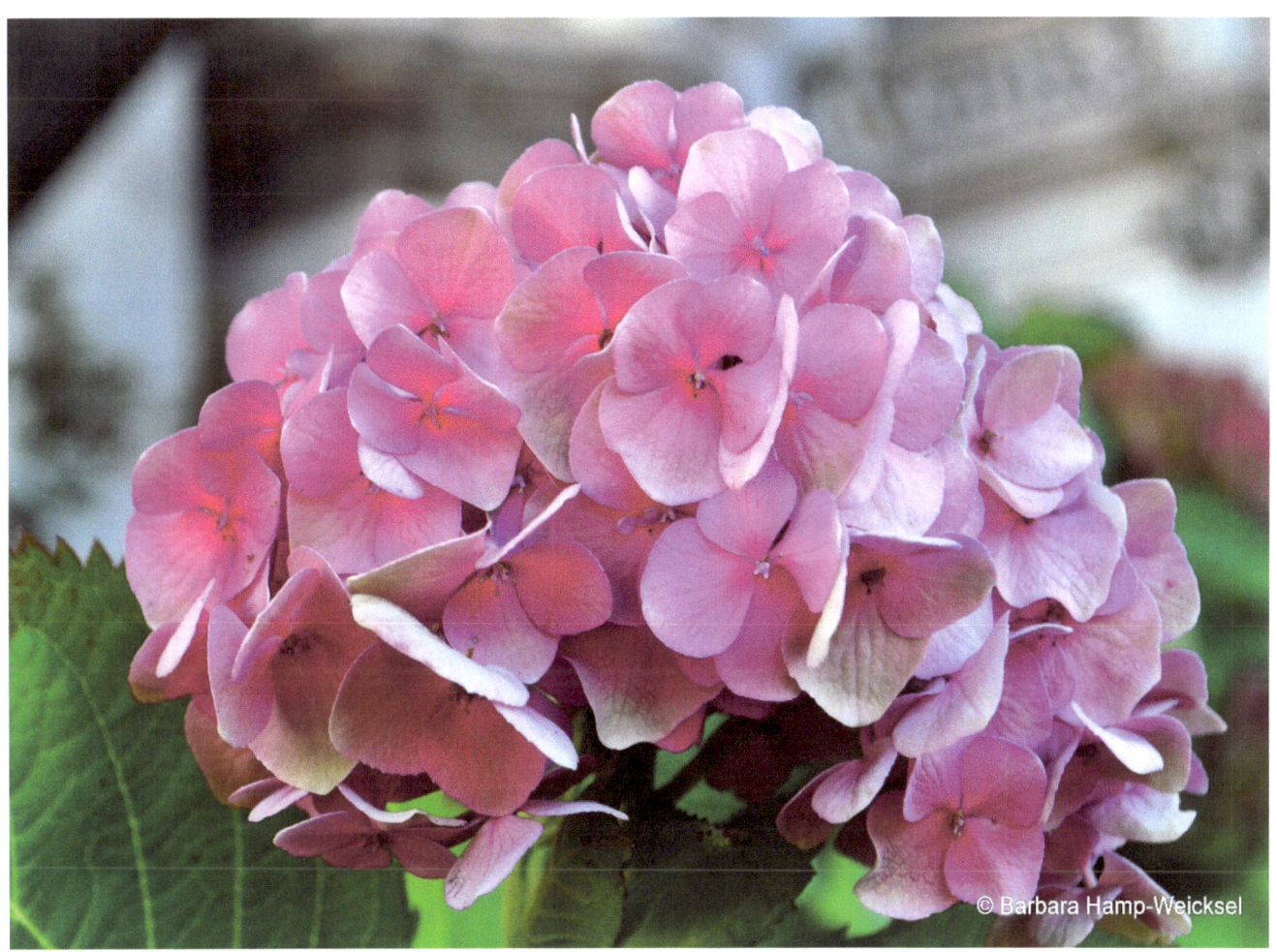

© Barbara Hamp-Weicksel

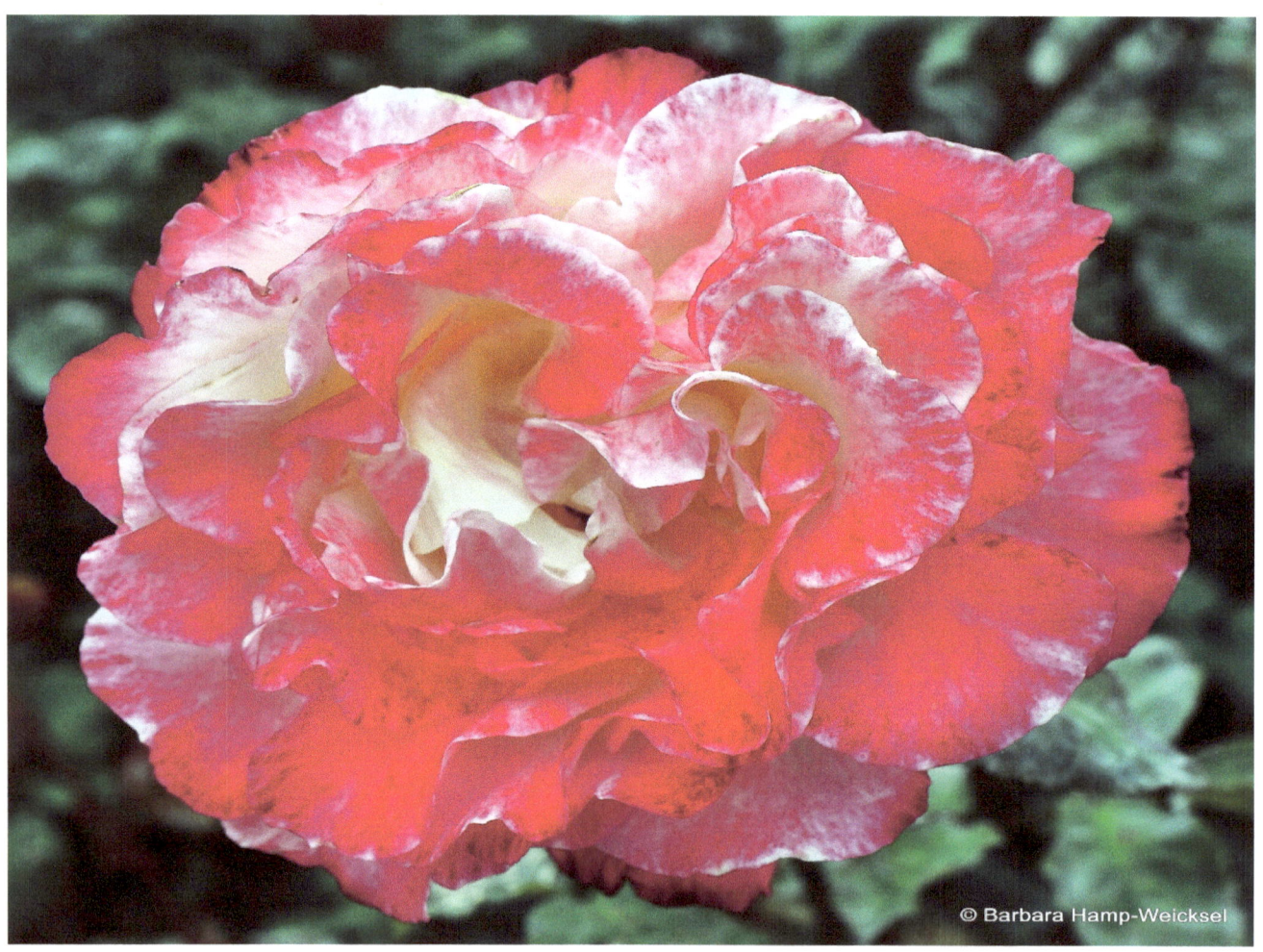

© Barbara Hamp-Weicksel

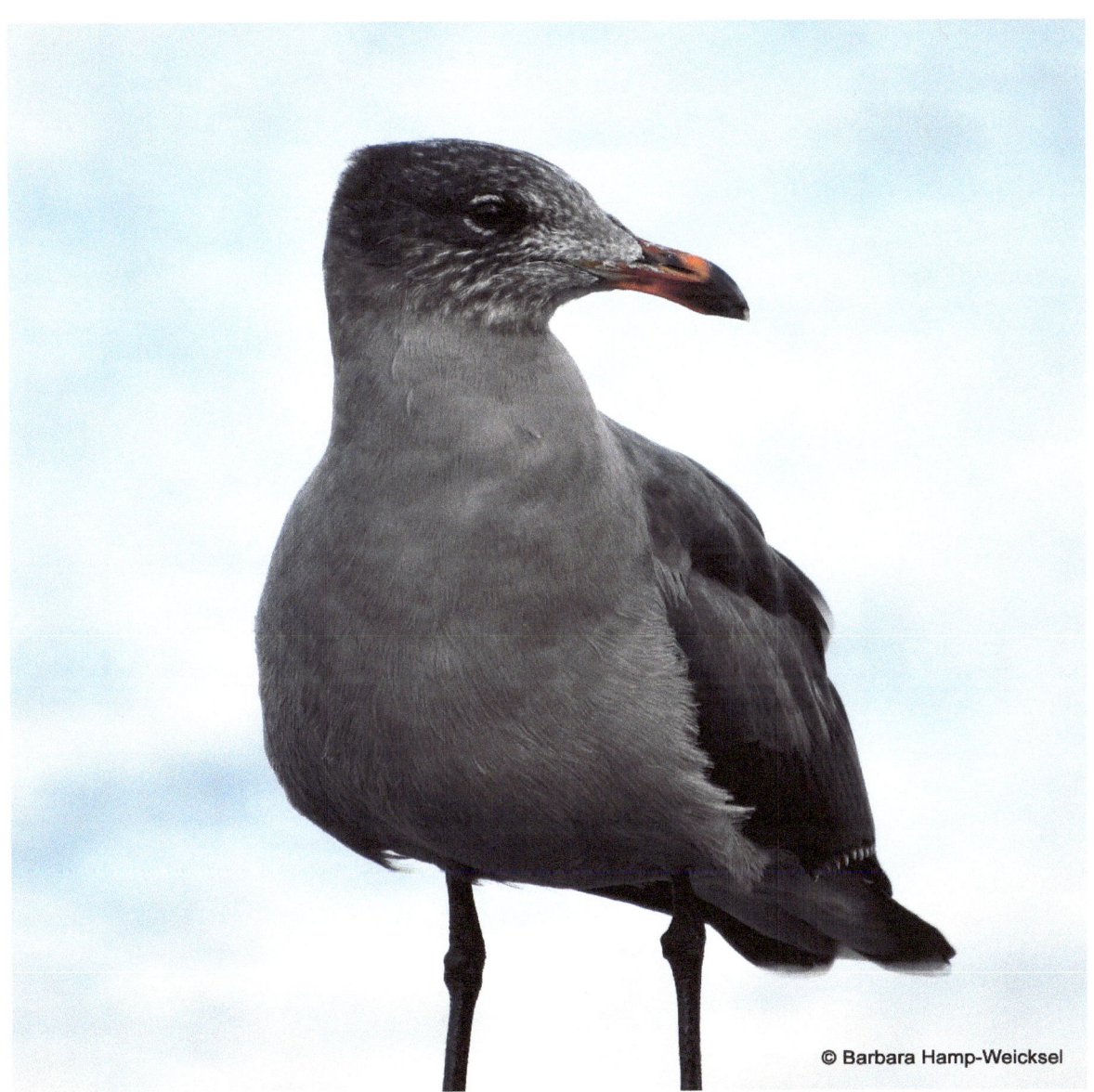

© Barbara Hamp-Weicksel

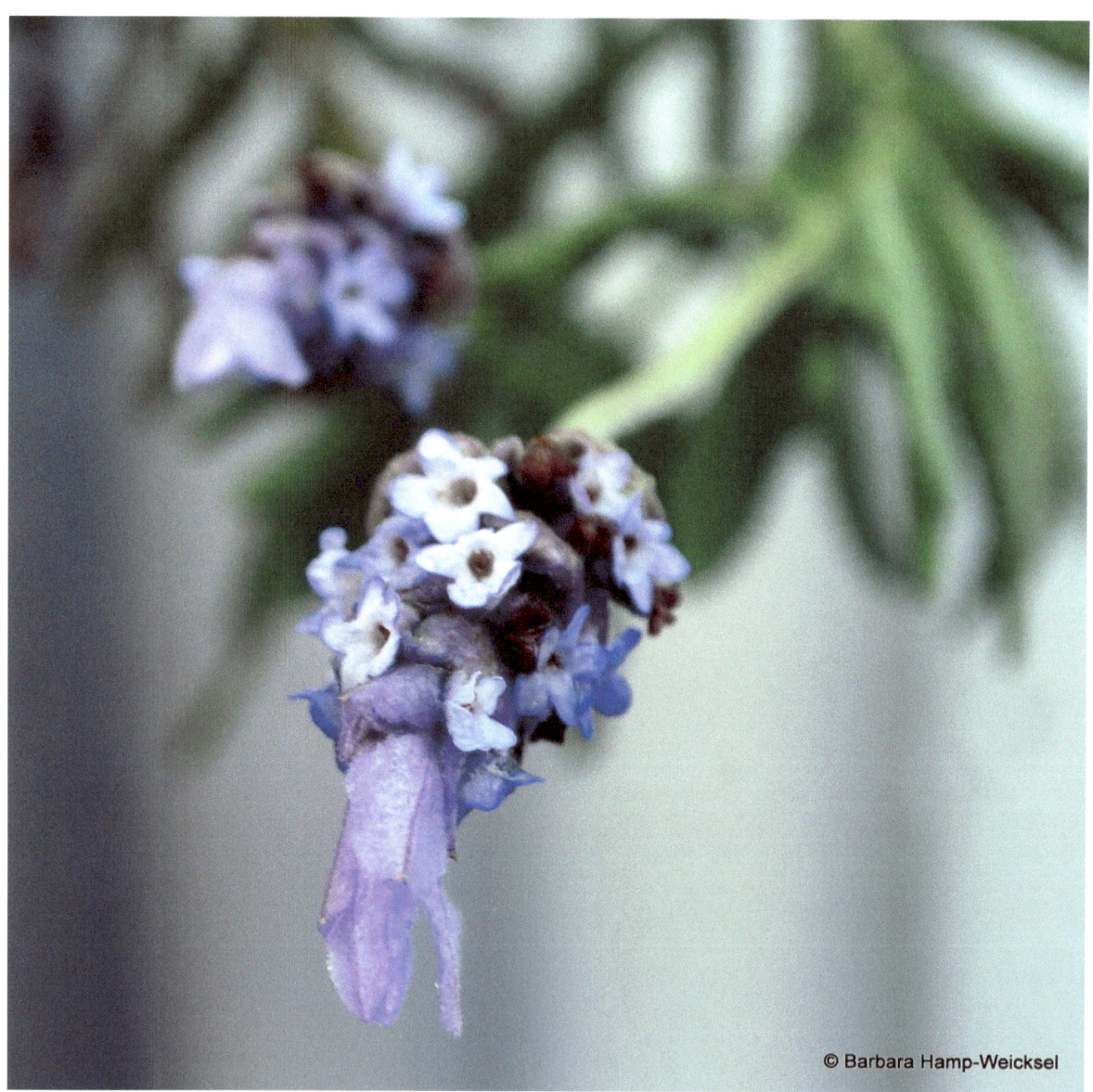

© Barbara Hamp-Weicksel

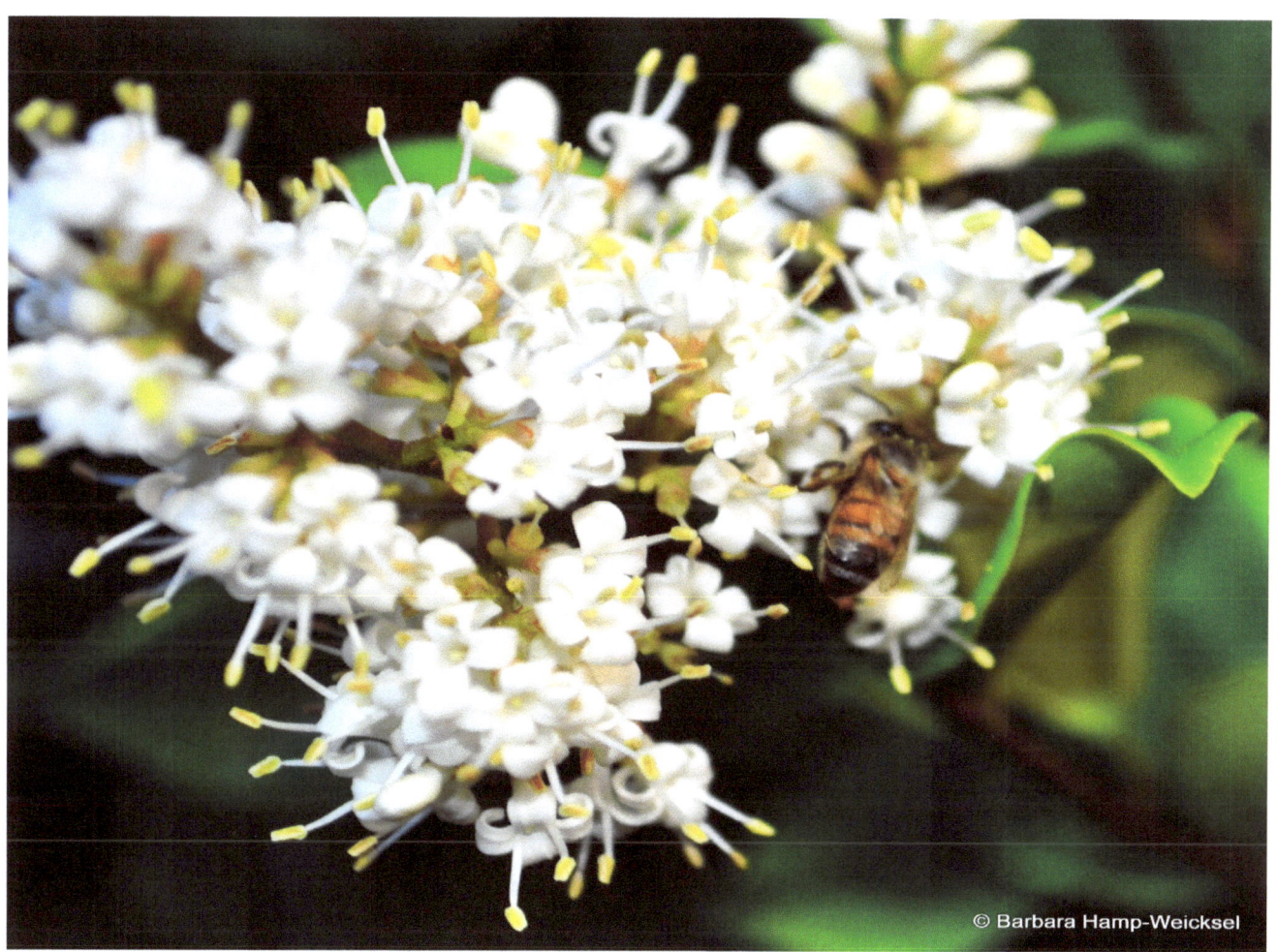

© Barbara Hamp-Weicksel

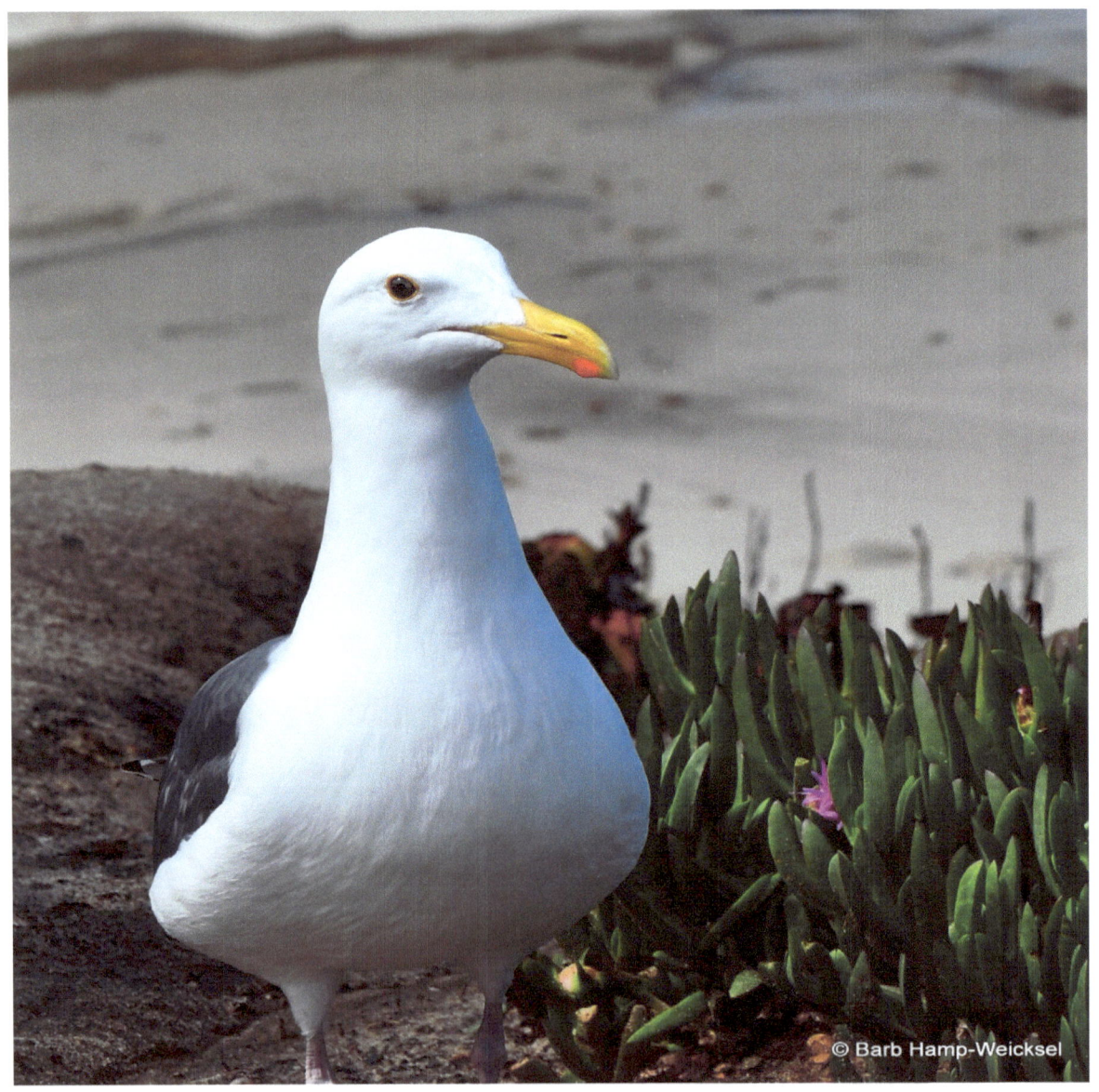

© Barb Hamp-Weicksel

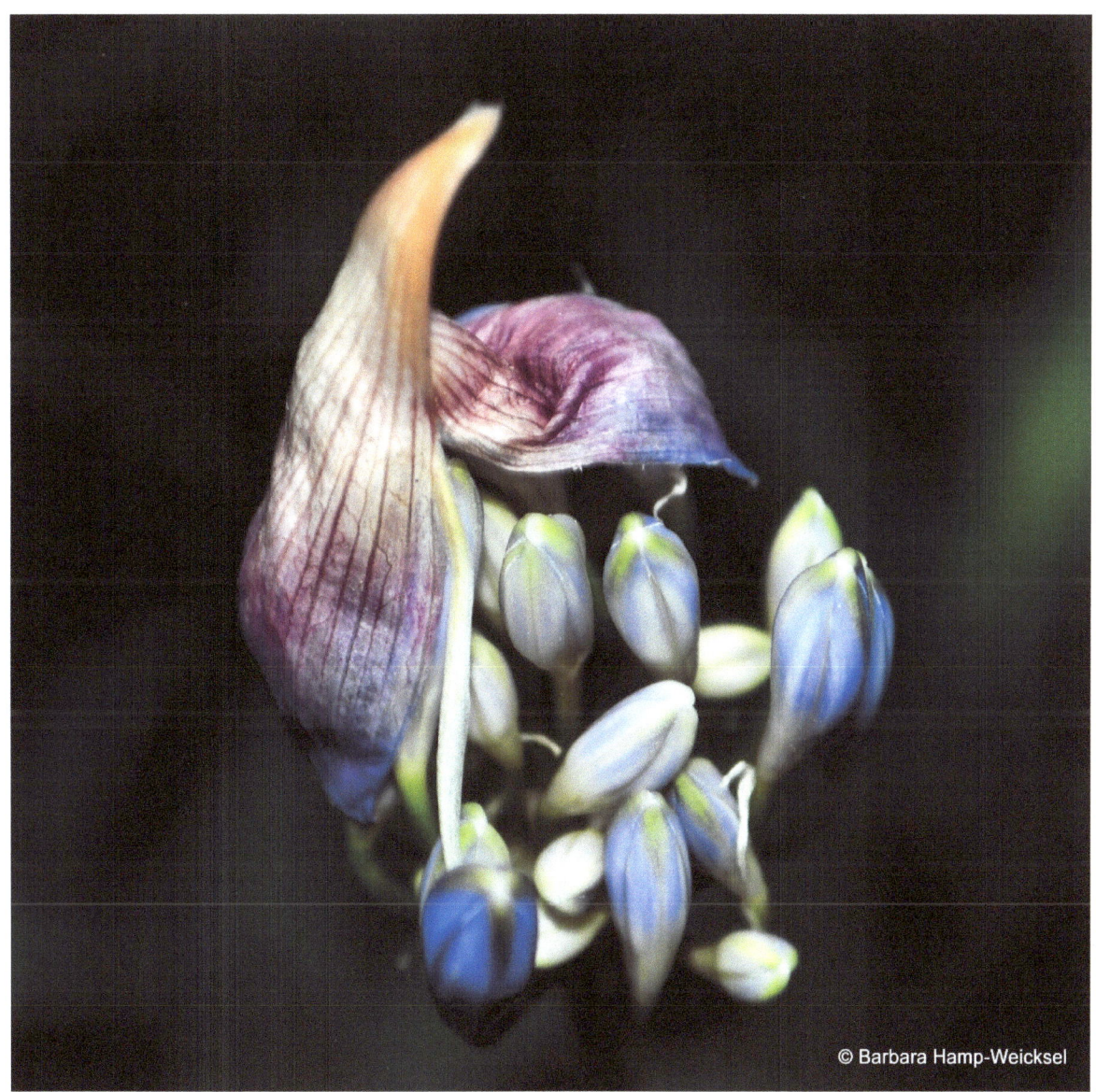

© Barbara Hamp-Weicksel

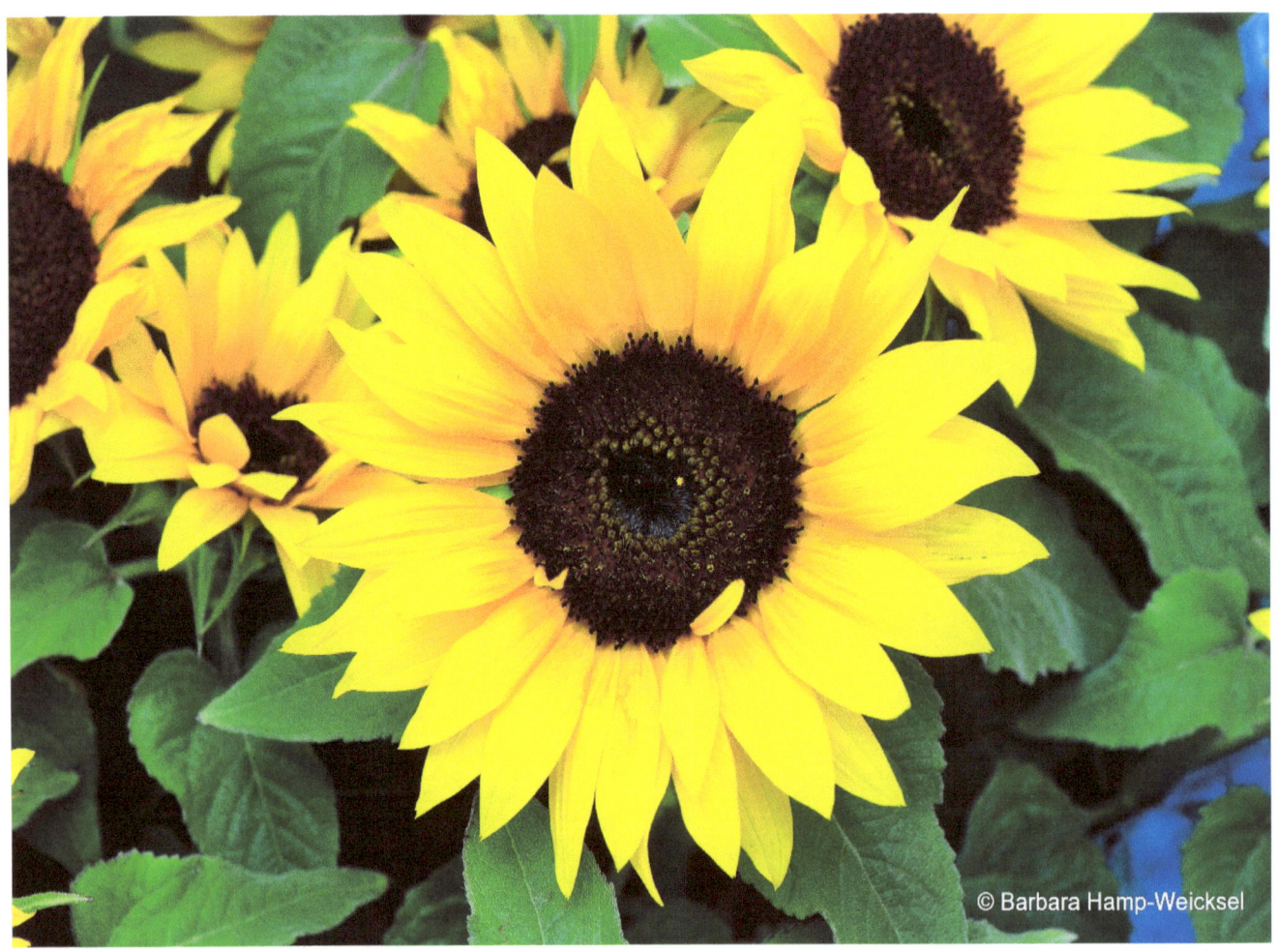

© Barbara Hamp-Weicksel

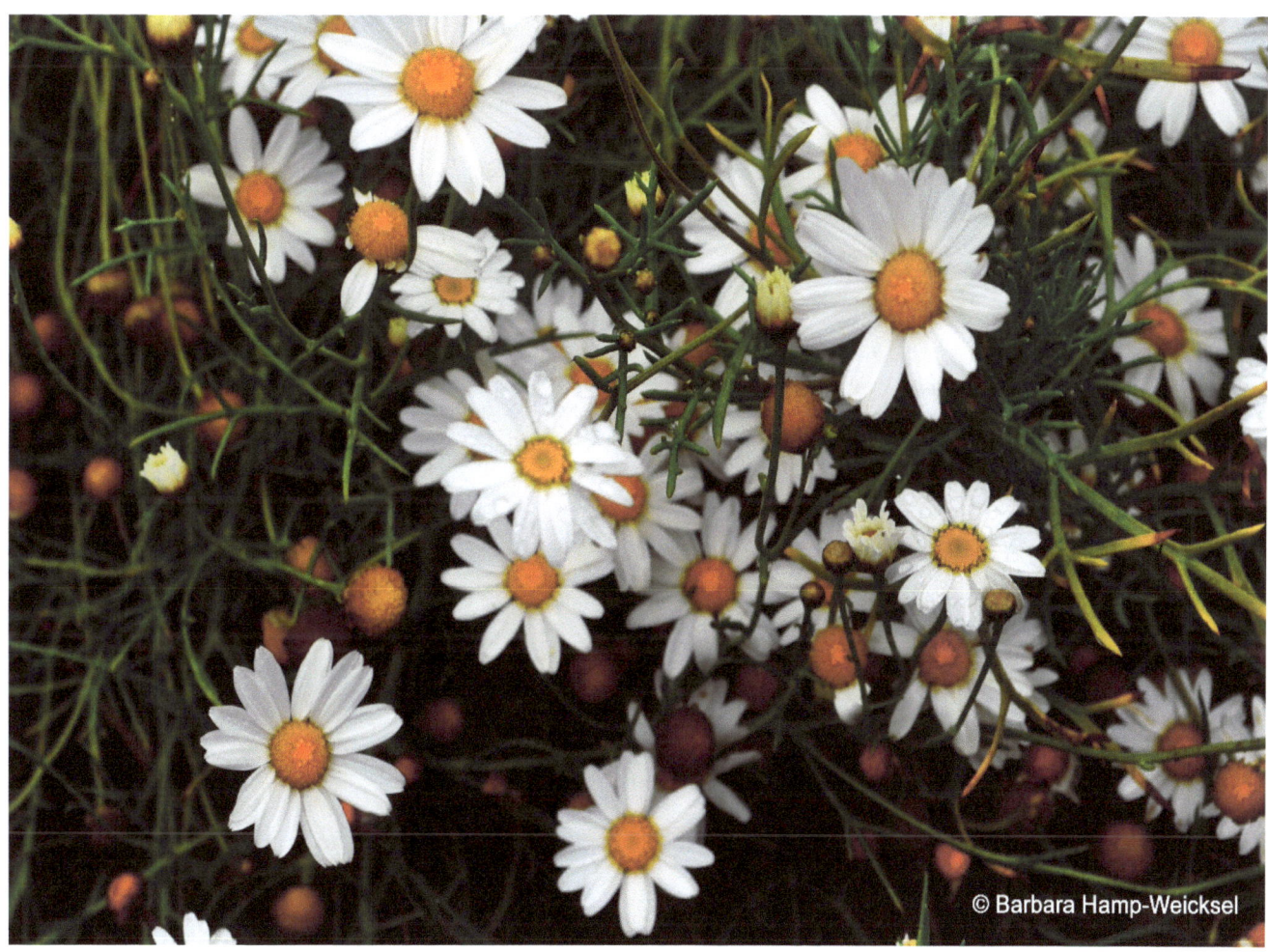

© Barbara Hamp-Weicksel

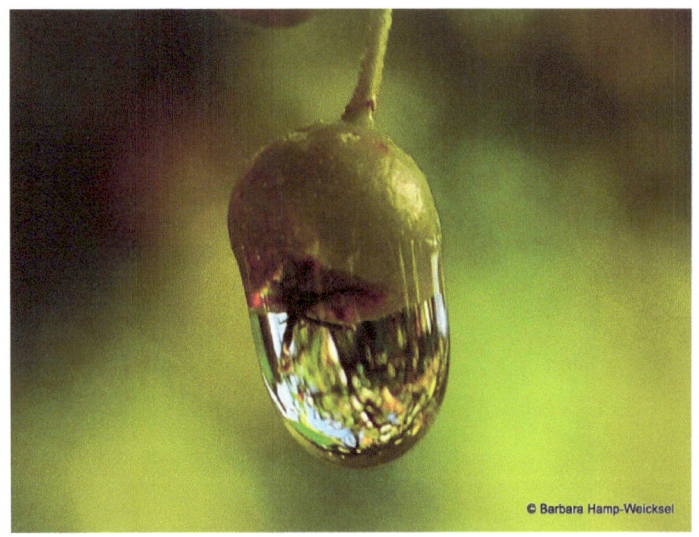

ABOUT THE AUTHOR

**Barbara Hamp-Weicksel lives happily in Southern California
with her partner, Susan.
She uses her Nikon D5000 Camera for all her photography.**

www.ingramcontent.com/pod-product-compliance
Lightning Source LLC
Chambersburg PA
CBHW050908180526
45159CB00007B/2827